Father's Day

Third Sunday in June

Father's Day, as we are used to celebrating it, is observed in both the United States and Canada. It began in the United States, but no one knows where it started or who started it. Some sources credit the holiday to Mrs. John Dowd of West Virginia, and others to Mrs. John Bruce Dodd of Seattle, Washington. Many people think it was started to make fathers feel just as important as all the mothers who are honored on Mother's Day, the second Sunday in May.

In the United States, it is customary for children to give gifts and cards to their fathers on Father's Day. In other countries such as Yugoslavia, children sneak up on their parents while they are sitting down and tie their feet to the chair legs. The parents must then pay a ransom in the form of a gift to the child in order to get untied. In North America, however, Father's Day is taken more seriously than that!

In fact, a national Father's Day Committee was founded in 1936. Each year this group meets in New York City to choose a Father of the Year. Many famous men have received this honor. Among them are Presidents Dwight D. Eisenhower and Harry S. Truman.

Making It Work

Have children write essays nominating their own fathers (or someone who is filling that role for them) for the honor of Father of the Year. Mount these essays attractively and encourage students to give them as Father's Day gifts.

Students can make a Father's Day collage as a personalized gift for their fathers. On heavy paper cut out profile silhouettes of a man's head. You might have several kinds, varying the hair style to provide for individual differences. Have students go through magazines and cut out pictures that pertain to their fathers' interests. Assemble a collage from the cut-outs and either use it for the gift itself or as decoration for the top of a gift box.

Brainstorm to make lists of all the special qualities of a good father. Discuss.

Run off copies of the Father's Day Certificate in this book. Students can fill them in, color them, and present them to their fathers (or paternal caretakers) on Father's Day.

Bibliography

Greenspun, Adele H.. *Daddies*. Putnam Publishing Corp., 1991.

Laulure, Denize. *Father and Son*. Putnam Publishing Corp., 1993.

Say, Allen. *Grandfather's Journey*. Houghton Mifflin, 1993.

Spier, Peter. *Father, May I Come?*. Doubleday, 1993.

Strangis, Joel. *Grandfather's Rock*. Houghton Mifflin, 1993.

Tompert, Ann. *Grandfather Tang's Story*. Crown Publishers, 1990.

Yolen, Jane. *Grandad Bill's Song*. Philomel, 1994.

Zolotow, Charlotte. *William's Doll*. HarperCollins, 1972.

A Perfect Father's Day

Author: Eve Bunting

Publisher: Clarion Books, 1991
(Canada, Thomas Allen & Sons; UK, Gollancz Services; Australia, Jacaranda Wiley)

Summary: This book tells the story of a little girl's unique perfect day that she plans for herself and her father to celebrate Father's Day.

Related Holiday: Father's Day is celebrated on the third Sunday in June as the day to recognize how special fathers are.

Related Poetry: "Mummy Slept Late and Daddy Fixed Breakfast" by John Ciardi and "Daddy Fell into the Pond" by Alfred Noyes, *The Random House Book of Poetry for Children* (Random House, 1983)

Related Songs: "Father's Day" by Kristine Wagoner, "D-A-D" by Debra Lindahl, and "Gifts for Dad" by Patricia Coyne, *Holiday Piggyback Songs* (Warren Publishing House, 1988)

Connecting Activities:

✦ Before beginning these activities, be aware that some children in your class may not have fathers in their lives, in which case they can focus on a grandfather, uncle, or family friend.

✦ After reading this book to your students, discuss the way in which Susie handled the perfect day, while allowing her dad to do a few things. Make a comparison chart to show the things that Susie did (go out to eat, ride on the toys at the park, get a balloon, etc.) and the things that Susie let her dad do (put her on the park toys, buy a balloon, drive, pay, etc.). Ask the children to decide who they would rather be, Susie or Dad.

✦ In the book, Susie planned the entire day for Dad. Make a list of Dad's favorite things to do and favorite places to go (fast food restaurant, duck pond, park, etc.). Have your students make a judgment as to whose favorite places they really were.

✦ Have your students evaluate the author's purpose in writing this book. Discuss why the author might have written this story and what its central theme is. Children might suggest ideas, such as ways to show fathers that they are loved. Have students identify what really made the day perfect for both Susie and Dad.

✦ Students may work in cooperative groups to create a story roll-up. Use a long piece of bulletin board paper. Each group of children can illustrate, in the correct sequence, one scene from the book (going out to lunch, the duck pond, the park, buying balloons, celebrating at home, etc.). When each group is finished, the long paper can be rolled up. To retell the story, slowly unroll the roll-up as the children in each group narrate the events in each picture. Save your story roll-up to share with fathers at a Father's Day Program.

A Perfect Father's Day *(cont.)*

✦ Since Susie and Dad visited her favorite restaurant, make a graph of your students' favorite restaurants. If possible, cut out the logo of each restaurant from advertisement material. If logos are not available, then simply write the name. Divide a large piece of tagboard into several equal columns, saving room at the top of the graph for the title "Our Favorite Restaurants." Place each restaurant at the bottom of the columns on your graph. You should leave one column free of names and label it "Other" to accommodate children whose choices may not be used again. Children may each place a sticky dot in the appropriate section to record their favorite restaurants. (These dots will come off the laminated surface if they are removed within a few days of doing the activity).

✦ Students may plan their own special day similar to Susie's day, to share with a father, grandfather, uncle, or friend. Each child should include his or her favorite place to visit and things to do. Children may then list their activities (with words and/or pictures) on a 12" x 24" (30 cm x 61 cm) piece of paper. Next to each activity place a blank clock face. On each clock face, have children add hands to show an approximate time when the activity should begin. A discussion of the length of time required for an activity will help your children record reasonable times. Title this sheet "A Perfect Day with _____" or "Our Perfect Father's Day." Roll up this sheet and tie it with a colorful ribbon as a special surprise for Dad.

✦ Students may paint portraits of their fathers to display on a bulletin board with a title, such as "Famous Dads from Room 3." Add a label to identify each father, such as "Jenna's Dad."

✦ Let children make greeting cards for their fathers on Father's Day. On the front cover of the card, children may draw a cake and add the number of candles needed to show how many years this person has been their father. Students may decorate their cards with items they think their dads would like for Father's Day and add suitable text.

✦ As a class make a class book called "Our Perfect Fathers" in the shape of a big necktie, using the pattern on the next page. Have each student do one page for the book in the same necktie shape, completing the sentence, "My father is perfect because ..." Attach the student pages to the cover and display the book during the culminating activity (see below).

✦ As a culminating activity, invite the fathers (or special guests) of your students to the classroom for a "Dad's Day" or short Father's Day program. Using the roll-up story, *A Perfect Father's Day,* look at the perfect days the children planned for their fathers, read a book together, make a picture together, do some manipulative math together, and finish the day with a "Perfect Dad's Party."

Class Book Cover

Directions: Color this page and mount it on a colorful piece of tagboard (making a border around the sheet). Use it as the cover for your class book of "Our Perfect Fathers."

Father's Day Certificate

This certifies that

_____

deserves to be honored on

Father's Day

June _____, 19_____

_____ _____

Signature   Date

Pencil Holder

Materials Needed: construction paper, crayons, scissors, glue, one soup can—cleaned and label removed

Directions:

1. Reproduce pattern pieces on white construction paper. Color and cut out all pieces.

2. Glue the "dad" rectangle on soup can.

3. Glue the arms to sides of the can. Fold them slightly forward for a better 3-D effect.

4. Glue legs to bottom of can. Legs can be bent to "sit" on edge of table or left flat.

Pencil Holder *(cont.)*

Helpful Coupons

Make coupons to give your father. On each coupon, write one thing you will do for him. Here are some ideas. You probably can think of many of your own ideas, too!

I will clean my room without being asked. (Good for one week.)

I will come the first time I am called. (Good for one day.)

I will make you breakfast this Sunday.

I will rake the leaves before dinner.

I will give you ten hugs sometime today.

I will not tease my brother or sister for three days.

I will do my house jobs cheerfully today.

I will draw you a special picture.

Here are some coupons you can use. Fill them in with things you know will make your father happy! Color them, cut them out, and give them to your dad.

Dad, you are the best!

_____

Dad, I will do this for you!

_____

A Special Picture

Draw a picture of yourself to give your father for Father's Day. Decorate the frame on this page. Cut out the inside section of the frame. Place your picture behind the frame, attaching it with tape. Cut a piece of colored tagboard to match the size of the frame and glue the edges of the frame and tagboard together.

Give yourself to your father!

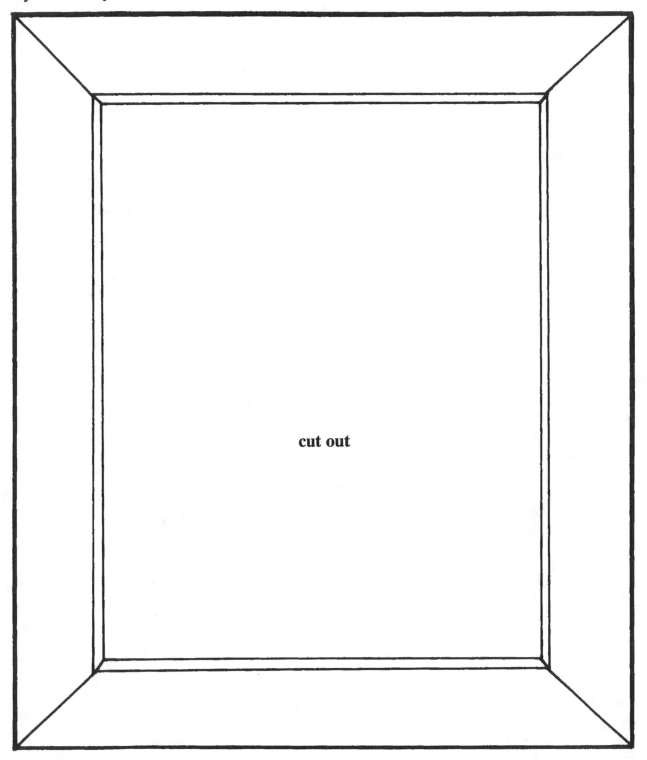

cut out

A Father's Day Feathered Friend

Here is an unusual card which is a great alternative to the traditional handprint.

Materials: 18" x 12" (46 cm x 30 cm) construction paper (folded in half, lengthwise), white tempera paint, black permanent marker, construction paper for beaks, two shallow pans, water, towel, glue, newspaper

Directions:

1. Spread newspaper out on floor.

2. Place folded construction paper on the newspaper.

3. Pour thin layer of white paint into one shallow pan.

4. Allow student to place bare foot into paint. Remove foot and press onto card at slight angle.

5. Let footprints dry while the student places his/her foot into a second shallow pan filled with water. Towel dry student's foot.

6. When paint is completely dry, allow the student to add bird "details" with marker.

7. Attach beaks with a thin line of glue.

8. Write a special message to Dad inside and give with a smile!

Duck Change Holder

Make this container for Dad to hold his change.

Materials: ½ lb. (.22 kg) small butter tub, white construction paper, crayons, scissors, glue

Directions:

1. Reproduce the pattern pieces on white construction paper. Color and cut out.

2. Glue water circle to the clear plastic butter tub cover.

3. Fold duck along broken lines and at the space between heads.

4. Glue duck together except tabs.

5. Glue tab A to C on water.

6. Glue tab B to D on water.

7. Curl grasses by wrapping or folding around a pencil.

8. Glue grasses to tabs A and B to cover them.

9. Put the cover on the tub.

Duck Change Holder *(cont.)*

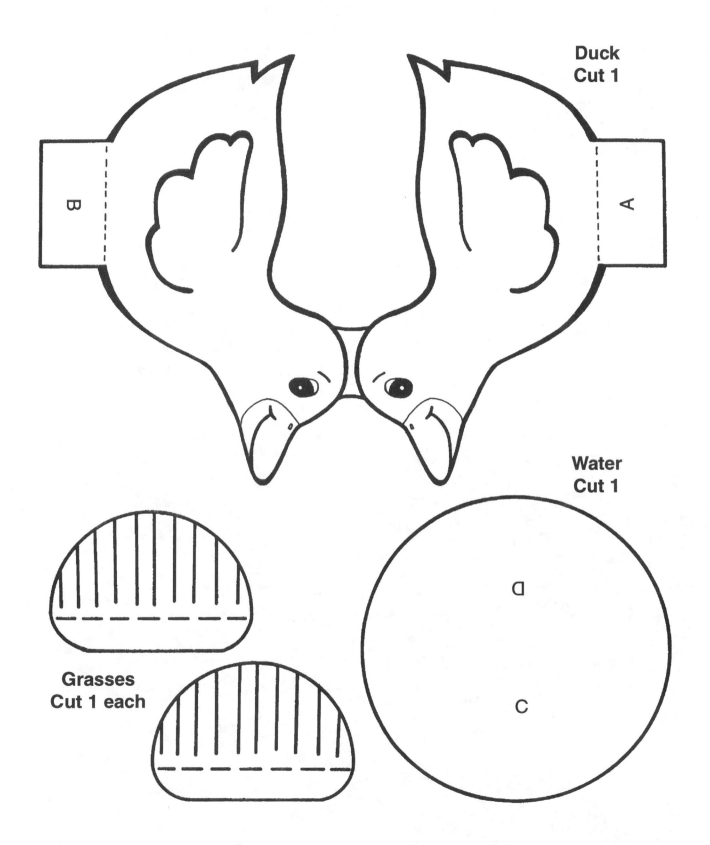

**Duck
Cut 1**

B

A

**Water
Cut 1**

D

C

**Grasses
Cut 1 each**

Father's Day Shirt and Tie Greeting

Materials: light blue construction paper, stapler or glue, scissors

Directions:

1. Reproduce patterns onto light blue construction paper.

2. Cut out each section of shirt.

3. Staple or paste upper and lower parts of shirt together.

4. Cut slits for collar and fold down on dotted lines.

5. Cut out pockets and paste on shirt, leaving tops of pockets open.

6. Write message on handkerchief, fold, and insert into one of the pockets.

7. Cut out tie and paste at top of shirt between collar points.

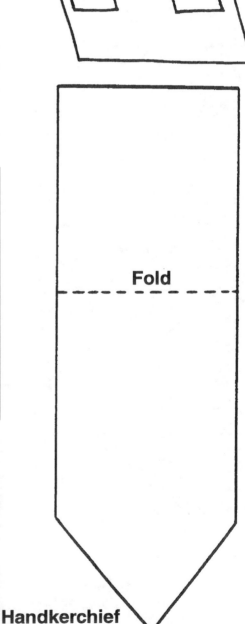

Fold

Handkerchief

Pockets

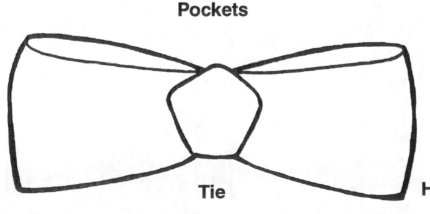

Tie

Father's Day Shirt and Tie Greeting *(cont.)*

Reproduce onto light blue construction paper.

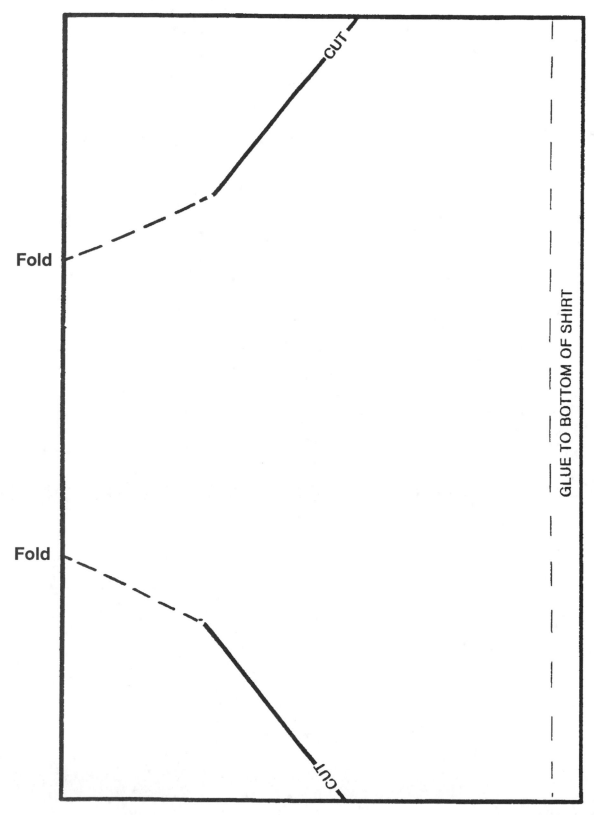

Father's Day Shirt and Tie Greeting *(cont.)*

Reproduce onto light blue construction paper.

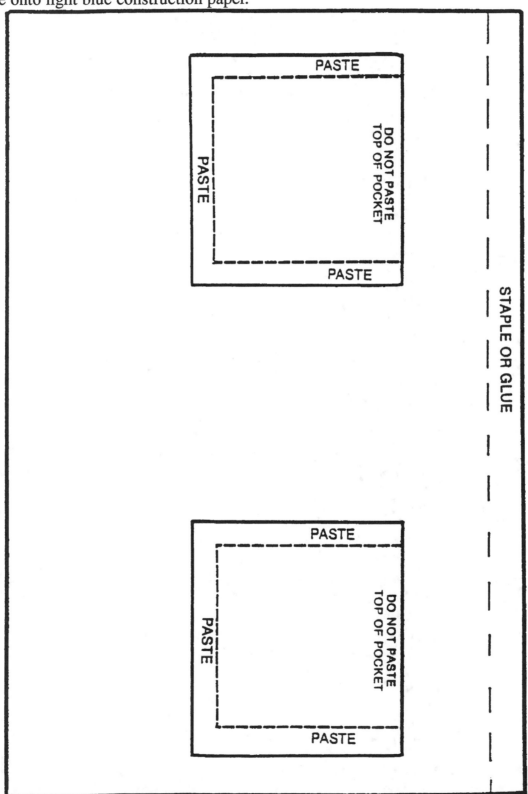

Junk Box

Give Dad his own box to hold all his "junk."

Materials: shoe boxes, materials for decorating boxes — markers, paint, paper or material scraps, pictures, cut-out letters, scissors, glue

Directions: Have students decorate the outside surfaces of the shoe box, including the lid. Have them personalize their junk boxes by adding their father's names or "Dad's Stuff," using the stencils below.